ABT

7/05

D0583424

Mummies

Inca Mummies:

Sacrifices and Rituals

by Michael Martin

Consultant:

Arthur C. Aufderheide, MD

Department of Pathology and Laboratory Medicine

University of Minnesota, Duluth

Capstone
press

Mankato, Minnesota

Edge Books are published by Capstone Press,
151 Good Counsel Drive, P.O. Box 669, Mankato, Minnesota 56002.
www.capstonepress.com

Library of Congress Cataloging-in-Publication Data
Martin, Michael, 1948–
    Inca mummies: sacrifices and rituals / by Michael Martin.
       p. cm.—(Edge books, mummies)
    Includes bibliographical references and index.
    ISBN 0-7368-3769-8 (hardcover)
    1. Incas—Peru—Túpac Amaru (Region)—Antiquities. 2. Mummies—Peru—
Túpac Amaru (Region) 3. Human remains (Archaeology)—Peru—Túpac Amaru
(Region) 4. Excavations (Archaeology)—Peru—Túpac Amaru (Region) 5. Puruchuco
Site (Peru) 6. Túpac Amaru (Peru: Region)—Antiquities. I. Title II. Series.
F3429.1.T8M37 2005
985'.25—dc22   2004010730

Summary: Describes Inca mummies found at Puruchuco and the ice mummies of the
Andes, as well as what scientists have learned from them.

Editorial Credits
Carrie A. Braulick, editor; Kia Adams, set designer; Jennifer Bergstrom, book designer;
    Kelly Garvin, photo researcher; Scott Thoms, photo editor

Photo Credits
Aurora/IPN/Ira Block, 4, 8, 10, 12, 13, 14, 17
Corbis/Charles & Josette Lenars, 25
Johan Reinhard, cover, 18, 20, 22, 23, 26, 28

Table of Contents

Features

Guillermo Cock (left) and other scientists found Inca mummies wrapped in cloth in Tupac Amaru.

Chapter One

A Race against Time

Guillermo Cock and his team of archaeologists had to hurry. They were digging in a small town in southwestern Peru called Tupac Amaru. The scientists believed as many as 10,000 Inca mummies could be buried there. The Inca were an American Indian tribe that once lived along the western coast of South America.

The scientists wanted to find as many mummies as they could. The town was growing. The building of new homes threatened to damage the mummies. Some mummies were already damaged by water seeping into the ground.

In July 2001, the scientists stopped their three-year project. By that time, the scientists had found the remains of about 2,000 people. Many of the bodies were preserved as mummies. Some well-preserved mummies still had hair, skin, and eyes. The scientists also found about 50,000 objects that once belonged to the Inca.

The Inca burial site in Tupac Amaru is called Puruchuco. It is one of the most exciting of all Inca discoveries. Archaeologists will be studying the many items found there for several years.

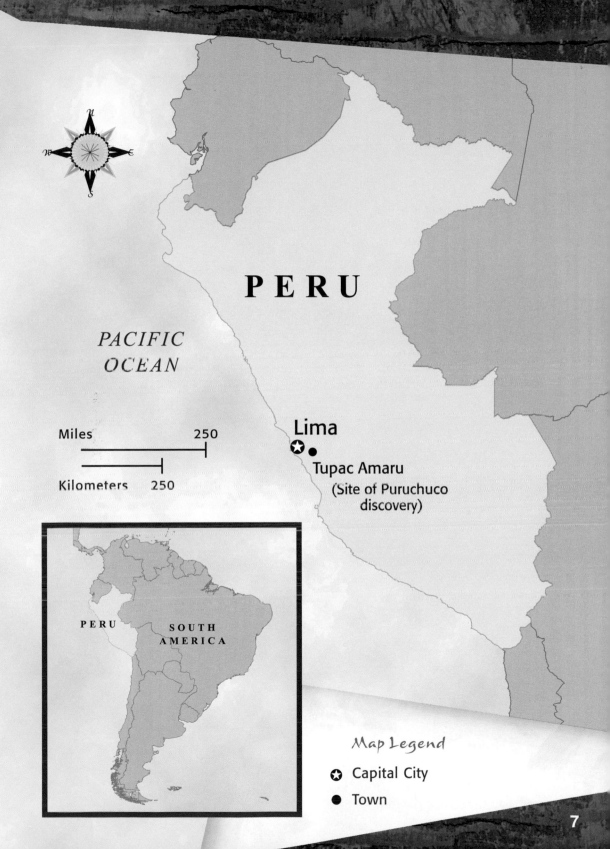

PERU

PACIFIC
OCEAN

Miles   250

Kilometers   250

Lima
Tupac Amaru
(Site of Puruchuco
discovery)

PERU   SOUTH
AMERICA

Map Legend

⊛ Capital City

● Town

The Inca wrapped some
bodies in cloth before
burying them.

8

The Inca

The Inca ruled the area along South America's western coast from about 1438 to 1535. The powerful tribe included about 12 million people.

The Inca buried bodies in the dry desert sand. They wrapped some dead bodies in cloth bundles before burying them. The sand probably dried the bodies to preserve them.

The Inca had strong religious beliefs. They worshipped several gods. They often killed animals as sacrifices to the gods. Sometimes, the Inca even killed children as sacrifices.

Puruchuco mummies that had headdresses were probably members of ruling families.

3 1833 04849 8197

Chapter Two

Digging at Puruchuco

Uncovering bodies and objects at Puruchuco was difficult for scientists. They could only dig in parks, schoolyards, and other open places. Pet dogs in Tupac Amaru often dug up the mummies. Scientists had to cover mummies with boards and rocks to keep the dogs away. Unclean conditions caused some scientists to become sick. Yet, the scientists continued because they knew their work was important.

Some bundles held mummies of children.

Bodies in Bundles

Scientists found at least 1,200 mummy bundles at Puruchuco. The bundles usually included several mummies wrapped in cotton and cloth. The bundles weighed as much as 400 pounds (180 kilograms).

Some bundles held adults and children. Family members may have been buried together. As many as seven bodies were wrapped inside a bundle.

The bundles were from the same time period. Scientists believe the bodies were buried there between 1480 and 1535.

Scientists have found Inca skulls in Peru that were cone-shaped. Many scientists think the Inca made this skull shape by binding cloth around people's heads.

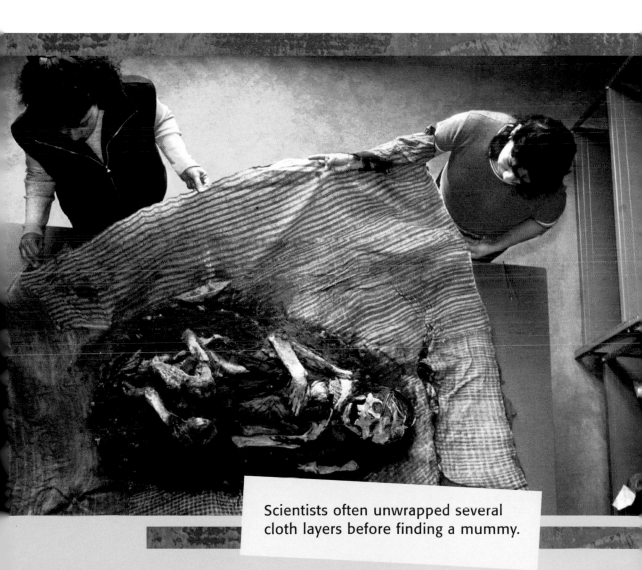

Scientists often unwrapped several cloth layers before finding a mummy.

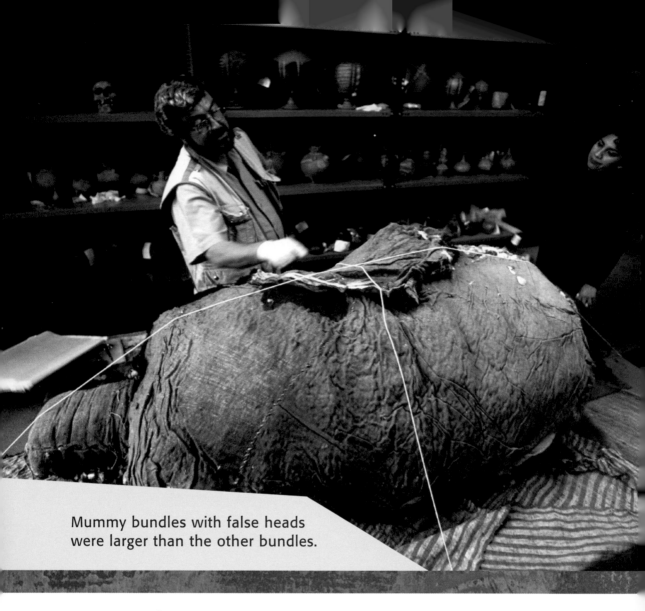

Mummy bundles with false heads were larger than the other bundles.

False Heads

Scientists found about 40 bundles with false heads at Puruchuco. Cloth-filled pouches had been placed on top of these bundles. Before these discoveries, only one other Inca mummy bundle with a false head had been found. The bundles with false heads were bigger than the other bundles. Some false heads had wigs or masks. Scientists think the Inca put false heads on the bundles to make them look more humanlike.

Archaeologists believe Inca leaders were inside the bundles that had false heads. These bundles were made of the finest materials. They contained headdresses with feathers. Headdresses were signs of power for the Inca. Scientists also found jewelry and warrior shields in the bundles with false heads.

Objects Left Behind

Mummies were not the only exciting discoveries at Puruchuco. Scientists found thousands of objects from the Inca. Many of the objects were wrapped inside the bundles. Some scientists believe the Inca placed the objects there so spirits of the dead people could use them. The Inca may have believed that a dead person's spirit continued to live in an afterlife.

EDGE FACT

Clothing was highly valued in Inca society. Textile artists were highly respected. The type of a person's clothing showed social rank. Rulers wore the finest clothing.

Scientists found many objects made by the Inca. They discovered clothing, pottery, and tools. Many tools were for making cloth. Scientists think many people buried at Puruchuco were textile artists who earned a living by making cloth.

Scientists also found food in mummy bundles. Corn was often wrapped with the mummies. It was one of the Inca's main crops.

The Cotton King

One mummy at Puruchuco was bundled in 300 pounds (136 kilograms) of cotton. Scientists named this mummy the Cotton King. Scientists spent several weeks unwrapping the Cotton King.

The objects scientists found with the Cotton King suggest he was an Inca ruler. The mummy's headband was made of bright, colorful feathers. Bright feathers were signs of high rank in Inca society. The mummy had sandals that wealthy Inca normally wore. Oyster shells in the wrappings were another sign of wealth.

A young child wrapped with the Cotton King is still a mystery. Scientists do not know why the child was there. They plan to perform tests to find out if the child was related to the Cotton King.

Cotton King

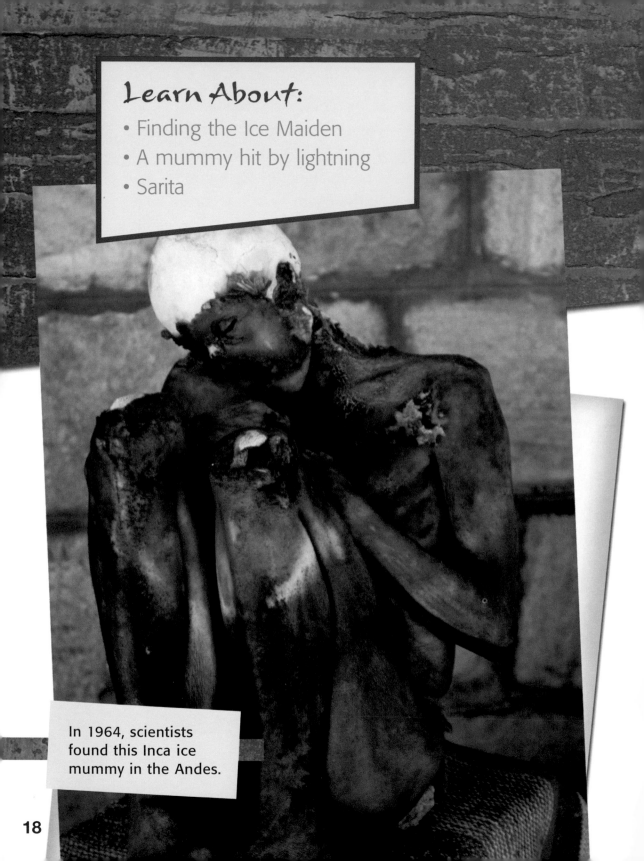

In 1964, scientists found this Inca ice mummy in the Andes.

Chapter Three

Inca Ice Mummies

The Spanish wrote stories about how the Inca sacrificed children to gods on mountains. Until 1954, some scientists thought the stories were just myths. That year, a child Inca ice mummy was discovered in the Andes. This mountain range stretches along South America's western coast. The mummy proved the Spanish stories were true. Since then, several Inca mummies have been found on cold mountaintops of the Andes.

EDGE FACT

Tissue from the Ice Maiden's stomach showed that she ate vegetables about six hours before she died.

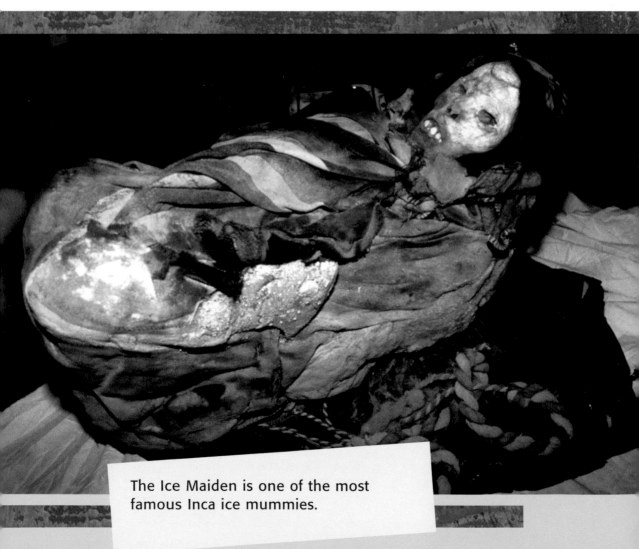

The Ice Maiden is one of the most famous Inca ice mummies.

The Ice Maiden

American scientist Johan Reinhard discovered the Ice Maiden in 1995. Reinhard and his assistant, Miguel Zárate, were climbing to the top of Mount Ampato in the Andes. Near the mountain's top, Zárate noticed something strange. Bright feathers stuck out of the ground. The feathers were attached to a small Inca statue.

The two men looked around. They found the ruins of an old stone structure. Farther down the slope, they saw an object that looked like a bundle. It was the well-preserved mummy of a young Inca girl.

Reinhard knew the discovery was important. He didn't want to leave the mummy unprotected on the mountain. He carried the 90-pound (41-kilogram) mummy down the mountain on his back. He brought the mummy to Arequipa, Peru. There, he placed it in a freezer. The Ice Maiden is one of the most well-preserved Inca ice mummies ever found.

Scientists carefully uncovered the Llullaillaco mummies.

Mount Llullaillaco Mummies

The Ice Maiden was just the first of Reinhard's famous Inca mummy discoveries. In 1999, Reinhard found the mummies of two girls and a boy on Mount Llullaillaco in the Andes. The mummies were buried under dirt about 5 feet (1.5 meters) deep. The children were between 8 and 14 when they died. The mummies were almost perfectly preserved.

Scientists believe one of the girl mummies had been struck by lightning. The strike had damaged one of the mummy's ears and a shoulder.

Scientists found objects with the mummies. They

Johan Reinhard (left) found the Llullaillaco mummies in 1999.

included clothing, gold and silver statues, pottery, and moccasins. *Time* magazine named the Llullaillaco discovery one of the 10 most important scientific discoveries of 1999.

Other Andes Discoveries

Some Inca ice mummies are not as well preserved as the Ice Maiden and the Llullaillaco mummies. But these mummies can still help scientists learn about the Inca. In 1996, Reinhard found an Inca mummy on Mount Sara Sara in the Andes. Scientists believe the child died from a blow to the head. They call the mummy Sarita.

Reinhard also has found Inca remains and objects on other mountains in the Andes. On Mount Quehuar, Reinhard found evidence that people had used dynamite to uncover Inca objects. The blast had damaged the human remains on the mountain. Reinhard found six bodies on Mount Misti. Scientists believe the bodies are Inca sacrifices. Reinhard also found silver and gold pots from the Inca there.

The Inca and Human Sacrifice

The Inca believed disasters occurred when the gods were unhappy. They thought an angry god could cause earthquakes, floods, droughts, and bad luck.

The Inca thought sacrifices made the gods happy. They often killed animals for the gods. They also offered the gods food and jewelry.

The Inca believed children were the most pleasing sacrifice to the gods. Child sacrifices were made on important occasions as well as after disasters. The Inca usually sacrificed children who were younger than 15 years old.

Scientists believe the Inca killed children in different ways. Clues suggest some were strangled, buried alive, or left to die in the cold. Some mummies show skull injuries. Scientists believe some of these children died from a blow to the head. The Ice Maiden may have died in this way.

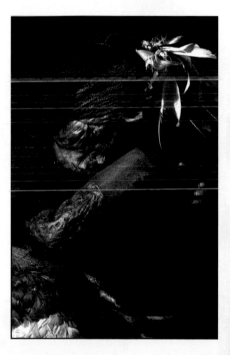

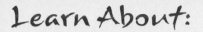

Learn About:
- Looking inside mummies
- DNA
- Recent discoveries

Scientists study mummies
to learn about the Inca.

Chapter Four

Mysteries Solved

Learning about the Inca has been hard for scientists. The Inca didn't have a written language. The lack of information about the Inca makes their mummies even more important. Mummies teach scientists about Inca life in several ways. They help scientists learn what clothing the Inca wore and the types of food they ate. Mummies also help scientists learn about diseases people suffered from hundreds of years ago.

X-rays and CT Scans

X-rays and CT scans show inside parts of mummies. They can show broken bones or the age of a person at death. Sometimes, scientists see jewelry or other objects inside mummy wrappings.

CT scans of the mummies from Mount Llullaillaco showed that their organs were preserved. The organs still held blood.

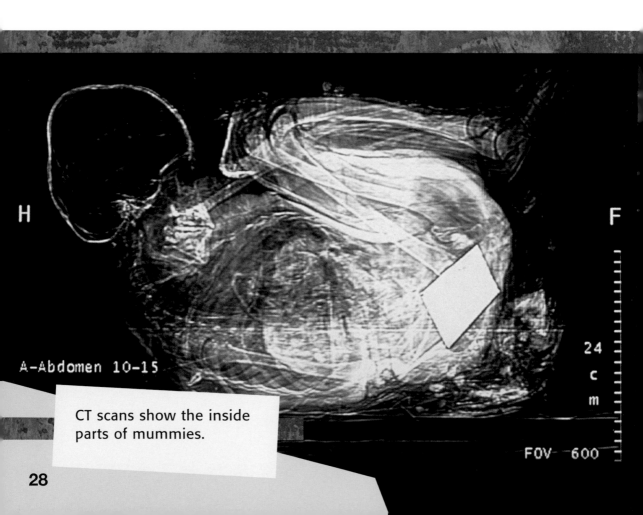

A-Abdomen 10-15

CT scans show the inside parts of mummies.

DNA

Testing the DNA of mummies is another way scientists can learn about the Inca. All living things have DNA in their cells. DNA forms physical features.

Frozen mummies often have preserved DNA. DNA tests can show the family history of mummies. The results also can identify modern-day relatives of mummies.

New Discoveries

Compared to other past societies, the Inca left little behind. Scientists continue to look for links to their distant past.

In 2004, scientists found Inca mummy bundles near Puruchuco. Tools found at the burial site are similar to those found in Puruchuco. They suggest that the bundles contain textile artists. This discovery and other future finds will give scientists a better understanding of people who lived long ago.

Glossary

archaeologist (ar-kee-OL-uh-jist)—a scientist who searches for and studies the items left behind by ancient people to learn about the past

headdress (HED-dress)—a decorative covering for the head

myth (MITH)—a false idea that many people believe

preserve (pree-ZURV)—to protect something so it stays in its original form

sacrifice (SAK-ruh-fysse)—the offering of something to a god

spirit (SPIHR-it)—the invisible part of a person that many people believe contains thoughts and feelings

textile (TEK-stile)—a fabric or cloth that has been woven or knitted

tissue (TISH-yoo)—a mass of cells that form a certain part or organ of a person, animal, or plant

x-ray (EKS-ray)—a picture that shows the inside of a body

Read More

MacDonald, Fiona. *Mysterious Mummies.* History Hunters. Milwaukee: Gareth Stevens, 2004.

Prior, Natalie Jane. *The Encyclopedia of Preserved People: Pickled, Frozen, and Mummified Corpses from around the World.* New York: Crown Publishers, 2003.

Takacs, Stefanie. *The Inca.* A True Book. New York: Children's Press, 2003.

Internet Sites

FactHound offers a safe, fun way to find Internet sites related to this book. All of the sites on FactHound have been researched by our staff.

Here's how:

1. Visit *www.facthound.com*
2. Type in this special code **073837698** for age-appropriate sites. Or enter a search word related to this book for a more general search.
3. Click on the **Fetch It** button.

FactHound will fetch the best sites for you!

Index